# Max's Bright Smile!

# What the book is about?

Max's Bright Smile is a heartwarming story about a boy named Max who has difficulty speaking. Despite this, he has a sweet smile, a kind personality, and a desire to work hard, which draws people to him.

Dedicated to my precious son.

Once upon a time, there was a special boy named Max.
He was special because when he tried to speak, his
words would get jumbled up!

However, Max didn't let this stop him from having fun!

Though he could not speak, Max had a sweet smile that could light up a room. He was kind and gentle, and he warmed everyone's hearts!

Max's family loved him very much. His mom, dad, and brother Mark were always there to support him and make sure he was happy!

They knew Max had a hard time expressing himself, but they could always tell how he was feeling by looking at him.

One day, Max's school was having a talent show.

All the children were excited to show off their skills!

Max was nervous. He wanted to participate, but how could he show his talent without speaking?

Max's mom had an idea! She knew that Max loved to paint! She suggested that he make a painting for the talent show.

Max loved the idea. He got to work right away!

Max spent hours painting.....

He chose bright colors! Bold Strokes! He expressed how he was feeling through his art!

When he was finished, he stepped back and admired his work. He knew his painting was beautiful. He was proud of it!

The day of the talent show arrived. All the children were excited! Max was nervous, but he had his family there to support him.

When it was his turn, Max slowly walked up to the stage. He was nervous, but he remembered that his family was there to support him!

He took a deep breath and unveiled his painting!

The audience gasped! It was a beautiful painting!

Max went back to his classroom feeling proud and happy. His friends and teachers came up to him, praising him for a job well done!

From that day on, Max's confidence grew. Even though he still had difficulty speaking, he found new ways to express himself through his art.

Max's story teaches us that everyone is special in their own way. We should never judge someone based on their abilities or disabilities.

Instead, we should embrace their differences and celebrate them. Max showed us that with hard work and a positive attitude, you can let your talent shine through!

Try out your own coloring and painting skills!

Try out your own coloring and painting skills!

Try out your own coloring and painting skills!

Printed in Great Britain
by Amazon

23745282R00016